# Why do we celebrate that?

Jane Wilcox

## CONTENTS

## FRANKLIN WATTS

### A Division of Grolier Publishing

LONDON • NEW YORK • HONG KONG • SYDNEY

DANBURY, CONNECTICUT

Being born is the first big event in anyone's life, even though the baby is too young to know what is going on. Parents often want to give thanks for a new child, and its safe birth. Religious ceremonies and traditional customs help introduce children to the duties and beliefs of the society into which they are born.

# BEING BORN

The Spartans of ancient Greece believed that babies were government property. Babies had to be strong enough to grow up to be warriors or healthy wives. Elders of the city inspected the newborn and ordered weak-looking babies to be placed outside the city to die.

## Christening

In the West, people are often christened in church when they are quite young. The service is a reminder of the baptism of Jesus in the Jordan River by John the Baptist.

At the christening, parents and chosen godparents undertake to bring up the child as a Christian. Holy water from the font is sprinkled three times on the baby's head, for each member of the Trinity: God the Father, the Son, and the Holy Spirit. A sign of the cross is made on the child's head with water.

Some Australian tribes used to knock out the two front teeth of their babies. Legend says that this was done by the good spirit, Muramura, to his own children, and the Australians carried on the tradition to please the tribal spirits.

▼

Muslims believe that a baby should be introduced to Islam very soon after it is born. At the Tahneek ceremony, a sweet is placed in the child's mouth to make the child kind and obedient. At the Ageegah ceremony, the baby's head is shaved and the baby is named. The cut hair is weighed and its weight in silver is given to charity or to the poor. Then a sheep or goat is sacrificed (two for a boy, one for a girl), cooked, and shared.

Jewish and Muslim boys are circumcised soon after birth, meaning a piece is cut from the penis foreskin. This is done by the Jews as a sign of their covenant, or agreement, with God.

The umbilical cord carries food and oxygen from the mother to the unborn child. This cord is sacred to some Buddhists, who preserve it in salt and bury it in a pot under two coconut trees.

Hindus believe in karma – that people are rewarded or punished for the things they do during their lifetimes. According to Hindu belief, the spirit lives forever, even though the person's body dies. The spirit is reborn in a new body that is either human or animal, depending on how good the person has been in the previous life. For example, someone who has been cruel to birds might be reborn as a bird in the next life.

In the Philippine Islands, there is a tradition that the mother and her newborn baby have to live near a specially built fire for a week. In order to purify the mother, water is poured over rocks heated by the fire.

Many Chinese believe that evil spirits can steal young babies away if they know the child's name. For this reason no name is given to the baby for thirty days. Then a feast is held and the baby is named.

Native Americans traditionally have names that describe some event in their childhood. For example, a member of the tribe might be called Broken Leg or Rides the Gray Mare.

Children are not considered full members of society because they don't know enough, and don't know right from wrong. Most cultures feel a need to celebrate the passage from childhood to adulthood. Ceremonies to mark this "coming of age" may involve physical pain or insults, or the child might make a vow to follow the society's rules. After this initiation ceremony, he or she is usually treated as an adult with new rights and duties.

# COMING OF AGE

For a Sikh boy to enter the Khalsa, or community of adults, he must go through a ceremony in a holy place. The Mul Mantra, which sums up Sikh beliefs, is chanted, and the young man drinks, and is sprinkled with, a special sweet concoction called "amrit." Members of the Khalsa must wear five special sacred things: the five Ks.

Kangha
(a comb)

Kesh
(uncut hair)

Kirpan
(a short,
curved sword)

Kara
(a steel bracelet)

Kachh (short
breeches)

In the past, young people weren't allowed a key to the door until they reached twenty-one. So getting a symbolic door key meant that a child had become an adult. Eighteen is now usually seen as the start of adulthood.

Under Jewish law, once boys and girls reach thirteen they are able to play an adult role in the life of the community and the synagogue. The ceremonies of Bar Mitzvah (boys) and Bat Mitzvah (girls) celebrate the passage to adulthood.

Most Christian churches hold a service of Confirmation for those in their early teens, when the vows ► made for them at their christening are confirmed. Confirmation is usually carried out by a bishop who places his hand on each child's head as they confirm their beliefs.

4

In East Africa, a Masai boy has to become a warrior as well as an adult. He must be brave enough to face lions and other tribal enemies. The boy's head is shaved, he takes a ritual bath and is then publicly circumcised with a sharp stone. He must not show any sign of pain or fear. After the ceremony, the boys grow their hair and dye it and their clothes with red clay.

Australian Aborigines traditionally go through a fiery initiation. They either walk through fire or have fire applied to their bodies. ▼

In the Taulipang tribe of South America, a boy is whipped and cut on the chin, arms, and feet. A bucket of stinging ants is held to his chest. The whipping is meant to purify him, the cuts make him an expert with the bow or the blow pipe, and the ants keep him always alert. If the boy shows any pain, he must go through the ordeal again. ▼

▲ Among Buddhists, there is no coming of age ceremony but it is common for boys between ten and twenty to spend time in a Buddhist monastery. In Burma, the boys reenact the story of Siddhartha, in which a luxury-loving prince became the Enlightened One.

Zoroastrians, whose faith originated in ancient Persia, have a ceremony called Naojote to initiate young people into their religion. The priest dresses the new member in a white garment called a "Sadre" and a thin girdle called a "Kusti." The Kusti has seventy-two strands of lamb's wool to represent the seventy-two chapters of their prayer book. As they pray the Kusti is tied around the waist three times, symbolizing good words, good thoughts, and good deeds.

# WEDDINGS

Marriage is the joining together of a man (the groom) and a woman (the bride) to make a couple who intend to stay together for the rest of their lives.

In a traditional Albanian wedding, the groom pretends to capture the bride, then takes her to his home where she has to stand in front of a fire. She has to hold a pair of tongs and cannot speak or sleep for three days. This symbolizes her dutiful promise to her new household. Then the groom gives the bride a leather belt to wear and the couple are considered married.

Before a wedding takes place in England, "banns" are read in the church for three weeks running. This is so that people will know of the coming marriage, and anyone who knows a reason why the couple should not marry has a chance to object. The bride's attire has three main symbols. White symbolizes purity. The bouquet of flowers symbolizes fertility. The ring goes on the third finger of the left hand because an ancient Greek belief was that a particular vein connected this finger with the heart.

Jewish weddings take place under a chuppah, or canopy, decorated with flowers. After the ceremony, the groom breaks a wine glass underfoot. This is a reminder of the destruction of Jewish temples by the Babylonians and the Romans.

### Wedding anniversaries

Wedding anniversaries are remembered each year on the date that the wedding took place. Traditionally, gifts of particular materials are given to the couple on certain key anniversaries:

| Material | Years |
| --- | --- |
| Paper: | 1 year |
| Wood: | 5 years |
| Tin: | 10 years |
| Silk: | 12 years |
| Crystal: | 15 years |
| China: | 20 years |
| Silver: | 25 years |
| Pearl: | 30 years |
| Ruby: | 40 years |
| Sapphire: | 45 years |
| Gold: | 50 years |
| Diamond: | 60 years |

In some Native American tribes, it was the custom for a woman to propose marriage. She did this by lighting a fire outside the man's tent and baking a cake. If the man ate the cake, the couple were considered engaged to be married.

Hindu marriages often take place in the house of the bride, who is dressed in red material with gold thread and wears gold jewelry and decorations of henna dye on her hands and feet. The elephant god Ganesha is worshiped by the couple on the day before the wedding.

Chinese weddings begin with an exchange of gifts between the two families and an agreement of the bride price. This sum is compensation for the bride's parents for the cost of bringing up the bride. Horoscopes are read to find out if the couple will be happily married. The ceremony takes place in the groom's house and consists of prayers and offerings to ancestors and the household gods.

The honeymoon is based on the ancient European tradition of drinking honey wine, or mead, for a month after the wedding. Attila the Hun (A.D. 406–453) is said to have died from drinking too much mead after his wedding.

In many Muslim marriages the man who performs the ceremony writes three copies of the wedding certificate. This is an agreement between the bride and the groom to follow the rules of marriage.

Spring festivals are often celebrations marking the end of winter. The arrival of new plants and the lengthening of the days were very important to early societies.

# SPRING

Purim is a celebration of the escape of the Jews from the evil clutches of Haman, the chief minister for the king of Persia, Ahasuerus. Haman wanted all the Jews enslaved or killed, starting with the proud and rebellious Mordecai. He began by building a gallows to hang Mordecai. However, King Ahasuerus was married to Mordecai's niece, Esther. She persuaded the king to have Haman hanged instead – and to make Mordecai the new chief minister. When the story is read to children, they hiss at Haman's name and eat cakes they call "Haman's purse" or "Haman's ears." ▼

▲

Palm Sunday marks the end of Lent (the 40 days before Christ was crucified) and the entry of Christ into Jerusalem. It was then the custom to wave palm branches in honor of holy visitors. These days, processions are held on Palm Sunday around or between churches with palms or crosses made from palm leaves.

Indian dancing is wonderfully expressive and Shivrati is a festival celebrating Shiva, the Lord of the Dance. It is held in the month of Phalguna (February – March). ▼

*An Indian devadasi, or temple dancer*

Good Friday, originally "God's Friday," is the day that Jesus was executed on a cross. Hot cross ► buns, now eaten throughout the Easter season, were first baked in England to be served on Good Friday. The buns have a cross made of icing on the top.

*A carnival costume*

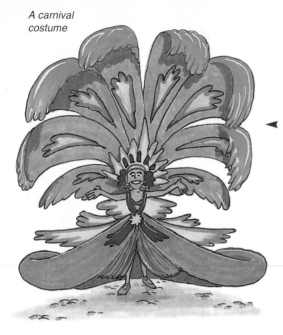

Many countries hold carnivals, often at the beginning of Lent. In New Orleans, the Mardi Gras was historically of special importance to black people, for at one time this was the only day on which black slaves were allowed to celebrate.

*Cherry blossom*

*Hollyhock*

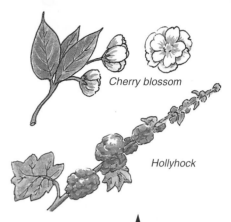

Many spring festivals are held in honor of flowers. The Japanese celebrate the Hollyhock Festival and the Cherry Blossom festival. They also celebrate Setsubun to mark the change of season. To drive out evil spirits, they place beans on a shrine and later scatter them around doorways and corners of the house. Small charms are placed over the doors.

The Feast of the Passover (Pesach), called a seder, celebrates the Exodus of the Jews from captivity in Egypt. They had no time to spare as they fled across the desert, so they baked bread without leavening it. It became the custom to remember this by eating unleavened bread, or matzoh, at Pesach. At the feast the youngest child asks four questions, which are answered by the father from his readings.

*Chinese lantern*

The Chinese hold the Feast of Lanterns in February to mark the end of their New Year celebrations. Lanterns are lit outside most buildings and huge paper dragons are carried through the streets.

The Hindu festival of Holi takes place in March as the trees blossom. It celebrates the story of a proud king who thought he was a god. The king's son would not believe this, and so his aunt Holika wanted him to be burned to death. However, the aunt herself finished up burned to a cinder. People light a big bonfire and then on the following day they throw water and colored powders at each other.

**9**

# SUMMER

Most ancient peoples understood that the Sun is the main source of energy for life on Earth. Although many summer festivals celebrate historical events, most of them are concerned with worshiping the Sun.

Building work on the great stone circle of Stonehenge began in around 2200 B.C. It was originally used to worship the Sun. On June 21, the rays of the Sun break over the horizon and shine on the altar stone. Recently, the celebrations of the old religion of the Celts have been revived there.

Tisha b'Av is a fast, and a sad festival, ► marking terrible events in Jewish history. In 586 B.C., Solomon's temple was destroyed along with much of Jerusalem. Later, in A.D. 135, a Jewish hero, Bar Kochba, and his men were massacred by the Romans. In 1290, King Edward I of England banned Jews from England, beginning a process which spread across western Europe. In 1492, 150,000 Jews were driven from their homes in Spain.

Beltane was a Celtic festival held on May 1 to celebrate the beginning of summer. Huge ► bonfires were lit in an effort to encourage the Sun to shine. Cattle were driven across the last flames of the bonfires to give the animals the holy strength of the Sun. Torches were carried in processions and burning wheels were rolled downhill.

In Sweden, the "endless" Midsummer's Day is of great importance. In ceremonies that go back to Viking times, people dance to music around gaily painted poles. They move in a clockwise direction, the direction the Sun appears to move through the sky in the northern hemisphere. Decorated ▼ maypoles are used in similar European traditions.

*English maypole*

In Japan, people celebrate Tanabaton on July 7 with fireworks and paper decorations. It recalls the story of a cowherd and a weaver who were so much in love that they couldn't do their jobs properly. The gods separated them and placed them at either end of the Milky Way. Because they were unhappy, however, the gods allowed them to be together on this one evening. ►

The ancient Aztecs of Mexico honored the supreme fire god, Xiuhtecuhtli, on August 1. He was also known as "He of the Yellow Face" and was important in Sun worship. His festival was called Xocotluetzi and involved the roasting-alive of slaves. However, there was also a jollier tradition of ► playing a game in which young people climbed greasy poles to win prizes.

*A modern version of the baptism ceremony* ▼

Whitsunday (Pentecost) is celebrated on the seventh Sunday after Easter, and celebrates the coming of the Holy Spirit to Christ's disciples. Some say "whit" refers to the "wit" or knowledge that made it possible for the disciples to preach in different languages. Others say it is called "whit" because everyone who was going to be baptized was dressed in white.

Some Native American tribes celebrated the middle of summer with a four-day "Sun Dance" around a pole. They took no food or drink during the dance. During the Okipa ceremony, dancers pierced their chests with wooden skewers attached by ropes to the center pole. They had to face the sun and dance without showing any pain.

In May and June, Sikhs remember the martyrdom of Guru Arjan Dev. He is seen as the apostle of peace and learning, and this period celebrates the victory of good over evil. Guru Arjan Dev built the Sikh Golden Temple at Amritsar, and wrote the Adi Granth, the Sikh Holy Book.

# FALL

Autumn is both a period of dying, as the summer ends, and a period full of life as late fruits and crops are gathered.

Divali is the Hindu Festival of Lights held in honor of Lakshmi, goddess of fortune and wealth, the wife of Vishnu. The festival lasts for a few days in autumn and is followed by the Hindu New Year's Day. Everything is cleaned and decorated and lights are placed in the window. Debts are paid, cards are exchanged, children get gifts, and plenty of food and sweets are eaten. ▼

Ganesh Chaturti is a celebration of Ganesha the elephant-headed son of Shiva who is the remover of obstacles. In south India it is thought by some to be unlucky to look at the Moon. One day Ganesh saw the new Moon reflected in the water and thought it was a sliver of coconut. When the Moon laughed at him, he cursed everyone who looked at her on this day. ▼

*Ganesha*

Asala Perahara is a great ten-day festival held in August at Kandy in Sri Lanka. It involves a vast procession of elephants, dancers, drummer boys, and torch bearers. A holy object, thought to be the Buddha's tooth, is also carried.

*The Buddha's tooth*

◄ October 31, the day before All Saints' Day, is called Halloween. It is the day when all the ghosts and spirits were said to be roaming about. An old Scottish prayer asks for deliverance from "ghoulies and ghosties, and long-legged beasties, and things that go bump in the night." Children in Britain and the United States sometimes go out to "trick or treat." They dress up as ghouls or witches, knock on people's doors, and offer people a choice. Either they must give the children a treat or a trick will be played on them. The children also carve jack-o-lanterns that often look very scary.

In September the Aztecs celebrated Teotleco, or the Arrival of the Gods, during which a strange ritual took place. The first god to arrive was supposed to be the one-legged god, Tezcatlipoca. Priests sat at the top of a pyramid with a bowl of flour set before them. On one special night a single footprint appeared in the flour as if by magic, showing that Tezcatlipoca had arrived.

The English celebrate Bonfire Night with fires and fireworks on November 5. This is to remember the execution of Guy Fawkes, a Catholic rebel who tried to blow up the Houses of Parliament with gunpowder in 1605. Traditionally, a dummy Guy Fawkes is burned.

Dusselbra, or Durga Puja, is one of the most popular Indian festivals. It falls in the autumn and lasts ten days, during which the goddess Durga is worshiped. She represents many things including war, love, beauty, and energy.

The Indian Parsees and Zoroastrians have a special autumn festival called Favardega during which their dead are remembered.

At the Moon Festival in mid autumn, the Chinese offer fruit and Moon cakes to the Moon goddess and the hare that lives on the Moon. The cakes recall the Chinese uprising against the Mongol emperors in the fourteenth century, because secret notes were passed inside cakes. The festival includes a lion dance and a lantern parade.

In China, the Double Ninth Kite Flying Ceremony goes back to an ancient story. The people were warned about a disaster that was about to occur, but only one man believed it. He took his family to the top of a mountain and flew to safety on a kite. They were the only ones to survive the disaster, so kite flying represents good fortune to this day.

Winter is the darkest and coldest season of the year. Food is often scarce in winter, though people have always enjoyed festivals of eating and drinking – perhaps to remind themselves that spring is not far away.

# *WINTER*

### Mid-winter madness

*The Romans celebrated Saturnalia in honor of the god Saturn. It was supposed to be a period of chaos between the old and new year when the normal rules of society could be ignored. People drank a lot, went wild, and gave presents to each other. Saturnalia was adopted by the Roman Christians and became Christmas, celebrated on December 25.*

For Christians, an important celebration is Christmas Day, which recalls the birth of the baby Jesus in a stable in Bethlehem. Jesus was visited by shepherds and three kings who brought gifts. Most of the modern, commercial Christmas activities have little to do with Christian beliefs.

Santa Claus was originally Saint Nicholas, a Turkish bishop imprisoned by the non-Christian Roman Emperor Diocletian. Saint Nicholas was said to be kind to children and the story is told that he once brought back to life three children who had been pickled in a tub.

Father Christmas may have been based on Odin, the Norse god, who wore a long white beard and a fur-trimmed cloak. He traveled the world on his eight-legged horse Sleipnir, making sure everyone was having fun.

The Norse celebrated Yule at the time when the Sun was at its weakest. The huge Yule log was taken into the house and burned throughout the festivities. Houses were hung with evergreen plants, such as holly and ivy, as a reminder of continuing life. Today, the Swedes also celebrate the Feast of St. Lucia on December 13. A young girl is chosen and she puts a wreath with seven lighted candles on her head. She has to get up early and take food to hospitals or the houses of her friends and family.

The Jewish festival of Hanukkah takes place in December. It celebrates the defeat of Syrian-Greek invaders by Judah the Maccabee in 165 B.C. The Jewish temple had been damaged by the invaders but was repaired and the menorah, an eight-branched candlestick, was re-lit. It is said that although there was only enough oil for one day, it stayed alight for eight. There are songs and prayers, and children play games of chance with spinning tops called dreidels.

*Menorah*

The Saturnalia tradition was kept alive during the Middle Ages when a winter Lord of Misrule was chosen from the peasant population. He was sometimes helped by a Queen of Misrule. They were also known as the King of the Bean and the Queen of the Pea. A pea and a bean were hidden in a cake and whoever got the slice with the pea and the bean became the King and Queen. The Lord of Misrule dressed up like a king and acted the fool, making fun of the local ruler and turning the normal social customs upside down.

The Celtic festival of Imbolc took place on February 1. This celebrated the end of winter and a prayer for crops in the coming spring. Corn dollies from the previous crop of grain were made.

*Traditional Mother Earth corn dolly*

The day after Christmas is Boxing Day. It got its name from the old custom of putting money for the poor in church collection boxes. Later, tradesmen and errand boys adopted the custom and some people still give money to the milkman, postman, or dustman for their service throughout the year. This holiday is celebrated primarily in England and Canada.

*Christian charity box*

FOR THE POOR

A year is the period of time it takes for the Earth to orbit the Sun. Any day of that year could be considered the start of the following year. However New Year's Day is commonly thought of as a day in winter – though the actual date varies according to local custom or religion.

# NEW YEAR

Rosh Hashanah is the Jewish New Year and occurs early in autumn. Faults and failures of the previous year are remembered solemnly. A ram's horn is blown for the service, recalling Abraham's sacrifice of a ram instead of his son Isaac.

Many people celebrate the beginning of the New Year. In Scotland, Hogmanay takes place on New Year's Eve and is an even bigger celebration than Christmas. Traditionally, people see the New Year in by joining hands and singing the song "Auld Lang Syne." There is also a Europe-wide tradition of first-footing (being the first to cross the threshold). Soon after New Year's Eve, someone pretending to be a tall dark stranger has to enter the house bringing a cake, a drink called "wassail," and a piece of coal for the fire. These symbolize good luck and prosperity in the coming year.

The Celtic New Year, on November 1, was called Samhain. The priests, called Druids, gathered a plant called mistletoe which grew on the sacred oak trees. Mistletoe was cut down with a golden sickle and was used as a medicine. It was thought by some people to help women become pregnant.

At the Japanese New Year, Buddhists ring the temple bell 108 times, a sacred number, so the year will be free of evil. For those who follow the older Shinto religion in Japan, the house is decorated with evergreens (for continuing life) and bamboo (for honesty).

*A torii is an ever-open gateway to each Shinto shrine*

*People still kiss under a sprig of mistletoe at Christmas and New Year.*

The Chinese New Year is the most important day of the Chinese calendar. In China itself, it tends to be a private celebration, but the Chinese in Britain and the United States hold big festivals in January or February. Many Chinese families keep a shrine dedicated to the Kitchen God who goes to heaven on New Year's Eve. There he reports on the family's conduct to the Jade Emperor, the god of the Taoist religion. The house is decorated with peach blossom and pictures of a carp and a fat baby, representing abundance and wealth, so that the Kitchen God will give a good report.

The day of Muharram is Islam's New Year, and commemorates the flight of Mohammed from his enemies in Mecca and his arrival in Medina. The Muslim calendar is calculated from this event which, measured on the Western calendar, occurred in A.D. 622.

In Japan, the New Year is marked by two festivals – the Greater and the Lesser. In the Greater Festival, prayers are offered to the dead, and friends exchange ritual gifts and visits. In the Lesser Festival, prayers for good crops are offered to the god of the rice paddy and a bird-scaring ritual takes place.

In the South Pacific region, great importance is attached to the appearance of the group of stars called the Pleiades in mid-October. This marks the end of the harvesting period and the end of the year. The festival of Makahki is held as a celebration. It is a time for feasting, sports, and truce-making.

# FARMING FESTIVALS

Late summer or autumn is the time for giving thanks for the harvest of the summer's crops. For many people it was, and still is, an important time because a poor harvest means a hungry winter.

*The Michaelmas Daisy usually blooms in late September*

Michaelmas (September 29) was an important day in the English farming calendar. This was the time when rents were paid and the hire of labor came to an end. It was also a time for feasting because it was at this time that farmers were paid for their crops.

In the United States, Thanksgiving Day is celebrated on the fourth Thursday in November. During the winter of 1621, half of the *Mayflower* passengers who settled in Plymouth died. The following fall, when their harvest was a success, the colony held a Thanksgiving celebration and invited the Native Americans to join them. It was made an official holiday by Abraham Lincoln in 1863.

The Jewish feast of Shavuot in spring is a celebration of the giving of the Ten Commandments to Moses on Mt. Sinai. It is also an agricultural festival when the synagogue is decorated with flowers and plants.

Sukkot falls five days after Yom Kippur and is a harvest festival. During the eight-day festival, tabernacles or booths are set up and meals, prayers, and readings take place. Fruit and vegetables are hung up. Four offerings are made of a citrus fruit, palm, myrtle, and willow, and seven circuits are made around the synagogue. On the last day, Simhat Torah, the year's readings of the Law are completed.

The Celtic festival of Lugnasad (August 1) was adapted and called Lammas by the Christian church. Lugnasad was a celebration of fruitfulness in which small sacrifices of food were offered to the gods. These celebrations were accompanied by sporting festivals and fairs during which marriage arrangements were made. Autumn is still a traditional time for fairs in Europe. ▲

In spring, festivals are held to celebrate the birth of farm animals and the growth of new crops. Easter in the Christian calendar was originally a pagan festival during which eggs were given as the symbol of new life. The Easter bunny comes from the hare that was the symbol of Eostre, the old goddess of spring. Eostre herself was based on the Babylonian fertility goddess Ishtar. ▼

*Easter bunnies on a German greeting card*

Christians in England used to celebrate the gathering of the harvest on Lammas Day. "Lammas" comes from the Old English word "hláfmæsse" meaning loaf-mass. Small loaves were baked from the first wheat gathered and were used in the Communion service at church. Traditionally, a corn dolly is made from the last sheaf of corn to be cut.

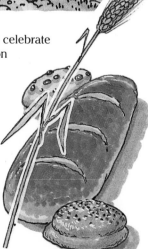

## Following the plow

The Roman historian Tacitus described a northern European Earth goddess called Nerthus. Her temple was on a sacred island in the Baltic Sea and her priests held a spring ceremony in her honor. Nerthus's statue and her chariot were washed in a holy lake by slaves who would then have to fall into the lake and drown as human sacrifices. ▼

Later, in mainland Europe, a cart in the shape of a ship was dedicated to Nerthus. It carried a plow as a plea for fertile soil in the coming year. ▼

The January Plow Monday festival is a Christian development of pagan plow rituals. In the Middle Ages, the farm plow was decorated with ribbons. It was followed by a jester and a man dressed as a woman who was traditionally called Betty. ▼

These days, where still remembered, the Plow Monday custom is for farm workers to go from house to house with a plow playing a sort of "trick or treat." Either householders give money to the local church or they have their doorsteps plowed up.

In simple farming communities, food becomes scarce during late winter and spring and it has to be carefully rationed. A period of hunger, or fasting, became part of religious custom – as did just the opposite, eating or feasting, to celebrate the availability of food. Fasting and feasting are often associated with pilgrimages, or journeys, to holy places.

Jesus spent forty days fasting in the desert before he entered Jerusalem to be crucified. This fasting before Easter is known to Christians as Lent.

# *FASTS, FEASTS, AND PILGRIMAGES*

The Sikh guru, Ram Das, founded the holy Indian city of Amritsar in the sixteenth century. The famous Golden Temple of Amritsar is the Sikhs' most holy place of pilgrimage.

Shrove Tuesday, or Pancake Day, is celebrated as the last day before Lent and was a chance to eat and drink well before going hungry. Pancakes were a special treat in which eggs, flour, and fat that would not keep for forty days were used up. Ash Wednesday is the first day of the fast of Lent. Sinners used to scatter ash on their heads as a way of showing their sorrow.

*In 1445, in Olney, England, one housewife was so busy making pancakes that when the church bells rang, she ran to the church carrying the pan because she was late. The villagers of Olney now hold a pancake race every year.*

Every week, Jews celebrate the Sabbath. It begins on Friday evening with a joyful service in the synagogue and then a family meal is set out with two candlesticks, a goblet of wine, and two twisted loaves, a reminder of the manna, or food, that the Israelites found in the wilderness.

Yom Kippur, the Day of Atonement, follows nine days after Rosh Hashanah. Many Jews fast from sundown the day before until the sun sets. Prayers for forgiveness are offered. The blowing of the shofar, or ram's horn, signals the end of Yom Kippur.

Ramadan is a month of prayer and fasting celebrating the time when God revealed the Muslim holy book, the Koran, to Mohammad. No food or drink is taken between sunrise and sunset on each day. The fast ends with a feast called Eid al-Fitr when new clothes are worn and cards are sent. The day is marked by acts of charity, prayers for the dead, a festive breakfast, visits, and gifts for children. The festival celebrates the glory and triumph of Allah and Mohammed's work in spreading the Muslim faith. ▼

The Hajj is a pilgrimage that every Muslim is expected to make during his or her lifetime, if they can. It includes visits to the Kaaba shrine at Mecca, to Medina, and to the mountains Sinai and Ararat.

Raksha Bandhan is a Hindu feast for brothers and sisters held in the month of Shravana (July – August). Girls tie red and gold threads around the wrists of their brothers, who promise to protect their sisters. ▶

In 1858, Mary, mother of Jesus, is believed to have made eighteen appearances to a young girl, Bernadette Soubirous, in a small cave in Lourdes, France. Bernadette was declared a saint in 1933 and the cave, or grotto, has become the world's greatest place of Christian pilgrimage. Miraculous cures are said to have taken place following visits to the grotto.

# BIRTHDAYS

In ancient societies, life was often hard and survival to old age was rare. Every year of life was a triumph over death, so birthday anniversaries were joyously celebrated. Birthdays are often marked with the giving of gifts, usually to the person having the birthday. However, in some societies, gifts are offered by the one whose birthday it is.

The birthday of Guru Nanak, the founder of the Sikh faith, is celebrated in November, though he may have been born in either October or April in 1469.

Elizabeth II, Queen of England, celebrates two birthdays. One is on April 21, her birth date. She also has an official birthday on the first or second Saturday in June. This official birthday is marked by the "Trooping of the Color," a ceremony in which the Queen's Household Guards go on parade. This traditional ceremony was started by King George II to celebrate the birthday of his grandson (later George III), and it continued into Queen Victoria's reign. However, Victoria was usually away on holiday on her actual birthday, on May 24, so she had the ceremony's dates changed to allow for an "official birthday" celebration to be held.

In China, each year is named after one of twelve animals, and it's said that everyone born in a particular year has characteristics of that year's animal. The Year of the Rat is the beginning of the present twelve-year cycle which started on 19th February 1996. This is followed by the Years of the Ox, Tiger, Rabbit, Dragon, Snake, Horse, Goat, Monkey, Rooster, Dog, and Pig. That means it will be the Year of the Rat again in the year 2008. You can work backward to find your birth year.

*The twelve Chinese years are...*

Monkey
(2004)

Dog
(2006)

Rat
(1996)

Pig
(2007)

Snake
(2001)

Horse
(2002)

Ram
(2003)

Rooster
(2005)

Rabbit
(1999)

Ox
(1997)

Dragon
(2000)

Tiger
(1998)

The Japanese have a Shinto birthday festival called Shichi-Go-San, which means "seven-five-three." All three-year-old children, as well as boys of five and girls of seven, are taken to the temple and given special sweets by the priest. Parents express their joy that their children have reached that age and pray for their wealth and happiness.

Burns' Day is celebrated by Scottish people on January 25 to celebrate the birth of the popular poet and songwriter Robert Burns. A key part of Burns' Day is the haggis. This is a sort of meaty pudding made from the innards of a cow or sheep mixed with suet and oatmeal. These ingredients are packed into the stomach lining of an animal and boiled. As it is brought into the room, bagpipes are played. Burns' poem *Ode to a Haggis* is recited before the haggis is eaten, and there is whiskey drinking, music, and dancing.

The Hindu festivals of Janmashtami and Ramanavami celebrate the birthdays of Krishna and Rama. These are two of the personalities of the god Vishnu.

Vishnu

Jesus Christ's birthday is celebrated on Christmas Day, December 25. However, some modern historians say that this must be wrong because the Christmas story involves shepherds watching their flocks by night. Traditionally, shepherds in the Holy Land did not allow their sheep to gaze freely until the beginning of April.

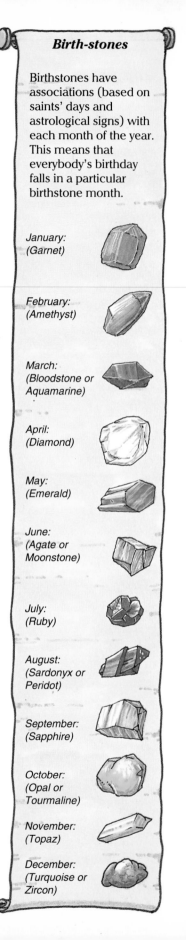

### Birth-stones

Birthstones have associations (based on saints' days and astrological signs) with each month of the year. This means that everybody's birthday falls in a particular birthstone month.

January:
(Garnet)

February:
(Amethyst)

March:
(Bloodstone or Aquamarine)

April:
(Diamond)

May:
(Emerald)

June:
(Agate or Moonstone)

July:
(Ruby)

August:
(Sardonyx or Peridot)

September:
(Sapphire)

October:
(Opal or Tourmaline)

November:
(Topaz)

December:
(Turquoise or Zircon)

As well as the births and deaths of holy people, their lives or actions are also celebrated on special days.

# HOLY PEOPLE

Saints are people considered holy by the Christian church. The lives of some well-known saints are remembered on particular days, but they can't all have their own day because there are about 4,500 of them. The Christian church sets aside November 1 as All Saints' Day so that all the saints can be celebrated. Saints are often shown with a halo round their heads.

Buddhism was founded by Gautama Siddhartha, an Indian prince, in about 652 B.C. He became known as the Buddha, or "Enlightened One" after seeing a vision of truth while sitting under a bo tree. His teachings have been carried to many countries, especially in the Far East where the main events of his life are celebrated in May by the festival of Wesak, or Vaisakhapuja. ▼

Saint George is the patron saint of Portugal and England, where his day is the April 23. He may have been a Christian soldier who was put to death by the Romans in Palestine in A.D. 303. He was very popular in the Middle Ages and his flag was carried by the Crusaders in the Holy Land. There is a story about him killing a dragon and rescuing a maiden.

◄ Patrick is the patron saint of Ireland and his day is celebrated on March 17. He was born in England in the fourth century A.D. but as a teenager was carried off to Ireland as a slave. Six years later he escaped and was taken by some sailors to Gaul (France) and returned home to England much changed. He went back to Ireland to convert the people to Christianity and built a monastery at Armagh. His emblem is the shamrock, a small Irish plant, and he is said to have driven the snakes out of Ireland.

Saint Swithin wanted to be buried outside his church rather than inside. When the monks moved his body into the church for his funeral on July 15, A.D. 971, a terrible storm blew up and the rain lasted for forty days. This resulted in a saying that rain on Saint Swithin's day will be followed by forty more days of rain. ▼

Apollonia was a Christian priestess in Alexandria. When the the Romans tried to punish her for her beliefs, they broke all the teeth in her jaws. Then they built a bonfire and threatened to throw her on it unless she gave up her beliefs. Instead, she jumped into the fire and died. Her day is February 9, and she is the patron saint of toothache. In a similar way, Saint Denys, who was beheaded, is now not only one of the the patron saints of France but also of headaches. ◀

*Ballet dancer*

Saint Vitus could cure people of diseases that make people lose control of their arms and legs. One of these diseases became known as Saint Vitus's dance, so Saint Vitus was taken up by actors and dancers as their patron saint. His feast day is on June 15.

*Haile Selassie*

Sikhs celebrate Baisakhi (usually on April 13) because Guru Nanak began his missionary travels on that day.

Baha'i followers send each other cards on 29th May. This is the date in 1844 when the Baha'i founder, Ali Mohammed, declared himself the Bab, or Gate of God. A later leader, Baha'u'llah, died on this day in 1863.

▼ Rastafarians celebrate the visit of the Emperor Haile Selassie of Ethiopia to Jamaica on April 25, 1966. Haile Selassie ruled the only African country never to have been completely colonized by Europeans, and he is revered as the living God.

Saint Roch caught the plague and was cured when he was brought food by a friendly dog. Although unable to cure himself, Saint Roch could cure others, and so became the patron saint of plagues. His feast day is the August 16.

# FANTASTIC FESTIVALS

Some festivals and customs seem so strange it's often hard to understand how they started in the first place. However, now that we have them, nobody seems to want to give them up!

Every twelve years, over ten million Hindus gather on the banks of the Ganges River to share in ritual bathing at the great Kumbh Mela festival at Allahabad.

Up-Helly-Aa is a January festival held in the Shetlands. A 30-foot-long Viking ship is built with a dragon's head and shields along the sides. After dark it is pulled to the seashore at the head of a torch-light procession led by a man called the Chief Guizer. Then the torches are thrown into the boat and the burning hulk is pushed out to sea.

WHO NOSE?!

Isn't Red Nose Day fun?! Every spring we get the chance to wear a silly red nose to raise money for the guys at Comic Relief. I'm glad that crazy bunch of British comedians thought it up! BUT... do you think we'll still be celebrating Red Nose Day in a hundred years' time?...

The Maori people of New Zealand used to practice cannibal sacrifices. The heart of the first member of their enemies to be killed in battle was offered to the god Tu–matavenga, the god of war. The heart, or if the person was important, the whole body, would then be eaten.

The Chinese Dragon Boat Festival has been held in early summer every year since the 3rd century B.C. Qu Yuan was a poet who drowned himself in protest at bad government. It is said that a kind of dumpling made of rice wrapped in bamboo leaves was thrown into the water for the fish to eat instead of Qu Yuan. Other people splashed the water to scare away the fish. Today, long, colorful boats with dragons' heads and tails race each other with a great deal of noise and splashing to celebrate the poet. The dumplings are still made too.

Well-dressing is an ancient Celtic tradition that continues to this day in some English villages. Originally the Celts honored the well goddesses by throwing a human skull into the well. These days wells are decorated, or dressed, in a Christian ceremony, with more pleasant objects such as flowers. It's said that no well-dressed well has ever run dry. ▶

April Fool's Day (April 1) is a day on which people play tricks on each other. The day is associated with the time of the first cuckoo, a bird that tricks other birds by laying its eggs in their nests. A traditional joke is to send a child to the corner shop to buy "some elbow grease" or "a left-handed screwdriver." Sometimes jokes are even played by newspapers or TV companies. A well respected British news program once featured an item about the "spaghetti tree harvest"! ▶

The biggest celebration ever will probably take place on New Year's Eve 2000 to see in not just the new year and the new century, but also the new millennium. However, non-mathematicians will probably celebrate the millennium a year early, on December 31, 1999!

In July, on the Feast of St. Fermin, the Spaniards of Pamplona hold a dangerous and dramatic festival. Bulls are allowed to run free through the streets while men and boys risk their lives to show their skill and daring by dodging among them.

Although death is usually a sad event for the family, many religions think of death as a new beginning, either in another world, or back in this one. Sometimes the dead person is thought to be joining his or her ancestors and this is a cause for celebration.

# DYING

The Parsees of India place their dead on a Tower of Silence where vultures are allowed to eat the flesh. The bones fall through a grid into a central well. Parsees believe in an event called Frashokereti when the dead of the world will be reborn and beauty and peace will reign.

*The Cenotaph*

▲

The ancient Romans believed in "Lemures", the spirits of the dead which were dangerous to the living. On May 9, 11, and 12 it was thought that a passage opened up between the world of the living and the Underworld. The festival of Lemuria was held on these dates to ward off evil spirits. The father of a household had to wash his hands then put black beans in his mouth and walk round the house spitting them out. Ghosts were supposed to follow behind picking up the beans. No one was allowed to look at the ghosts until the ceremony had been completed nine times. The bean-spitter finally chanted, "Shades of my fathers depart" nine times, and could then look to see if the ghosts had gone. They usually had!

▲

Remembrance Sunday is the day on which British and Commonwealth people remember the dead of the two World Wars. On the second Saturday in November, there is a special ceremony in the Albert Hall in London with military music, prayers, and a procession of veterans and flags. Similarly, in the U.S., Veterans Day is celebrated on November 11, usually with parades and services.

▲ The Aztecs made daily human sacrifices to the Sun god, Tonatiuh. Victims were happy to die and go to the "'Land of the Dead" because they believed that they would join an eternal, holy fire. The human sacrifices were carried to the top of a pyramid where their hearts were cut out and offered to the Sun. The dead bodies were thrown down the steps of the pyramid that would run red with blood.

When a close member of the family or a friend has died, Orthodox Jews say "Blessed be the true Judge." They tear part of their clothes as a symbol of their grief and go into strict mourning for seven days (called shivah), staying at home, wearing no shoes and sitting on a low stool. There follows a month of general mourning until a stone has been laid on the grave. ▶

Many Chinese people believe that the dead continue to watch over their descendants from "The Land of Shades." They also think that the soul of someone who dies will be judged and perhaps punished. For this reason the Chinese celebrate Yu lan-p'en, when they burn specially made paper gifts such as money, houses, or even cars. It's thought that these can then be taken to the next life where they may be useful to the person who has died. The body is buried with a lot of loud noises and fireworks to scare off the evil spirits. Ten years after the burial, the bones are dug up, cleaned, and planted in a pot which is then buried at a new, carefully selected site. A special carved tomb is made, which the family visits during the Ch'ing Ming festival.

The Hindus cremate their dead because they believe that the soul no longer needs the body after death. They also think that a dead body is polluted and unclean, so most mourners don't touch other people until the ceremonies are finished. The body is burned on a pyre of wood as prayers and readings take place. Three days later, the ashes are collected and scattered in a river, preferably the sacred Ganges River. Ten or eleven days later, offerings of rice balls are made to those who died and also to other dead relatives. After this, the family members are thought to be clean once more.

The Sikhs believe in the rebirth of the soul and are not supposed to feel sad about death. The body of the dead person is washed and dressed and taken to the Temple. After the cremation, the ashes are scattered with flowers onto a running stream. For the following ten days the Adi Granth (the Sikh holy book) is read.

In many religions the relatives and friends of a dead person hold a wake, during which people stay up with the body to watch over it until it is buried. This was originally done to make sure the "body" was really dead, so avoiding burying a person alive by mistake. A traditional Irish wake is a lively occasion with a great deal of drinking and feasting that can last for days.

Most countries celebrate important days and events in their history – such as a revolution or gaining independence. National holidays are usually encouraged by governments as a way of maintaining national pride. They are often marked by a day off work or school.

# NATIONAL HOLIDAYS

The Swiss celebrate their Independence Day on August 1, the date in 1291 when the Everlasting League was formed to resist the Austrian occupation of Switzerland. ▼

On July 14, 1789, French revolutionaries stormed the Bastille prison in Paris and released the prisoners. Bastille Day is celebrated on this date to mark the start of the French Revolution.

July 4 is celebrated as Independence Day in the U.S. This date marks the breaking away of the original thirteen colonies from British rule in 1776. In many towns across the country, people put on parades, barbecues, picnics, pageants, and firework displays. ▶

▲ The Peruvians celebrate their Independence Day on December 9. This is the date in 1824 when the revolutionaries Simon Bolívar and General Antonio Jose de Sucre defeated the Spanish army at the battles of Junin and Ayacucho.

Several Latin American countries recognize Columbus Day, ▶ October 12, when the explorer Christopher Columbus sighted American land in 1492.

October 24 has been set aside for all countries to celebrate United Nations Day. The ▶ United Nations is an organization set up in 1945 to try to resolve differences between nations and peoples all over the world.

*United Nations flag*

# COLIN'S CRAZY CALENDAR

Colin has a problem. Some of his descriptions of ceremonies and festivals have become mixed up. Can you tell him which first lines should go with which second lines?...

QUIZ

1. Norsemen thought that Odin traveled the world
2. in order to win prizes.

3. On New Year's Eve, a tall dark stranger may come,
4. to stand near the fire for the next three days.

5. On April Fool's Day, a fool might try
6. riding an eight-legged horse called Sleipnir.

7. Some ancient Aztecs climbed greasy poles
8. to watch the sun rise over Stonehenge.

9. After a traditional Albanian wedding the bride had
10. the boat-burning festival of Up-Helly-Aa.

11. The patron saint of headaches is
12. bringing in a lucky lump of coal.

13. In January, Shetland Islanders may visit
14. St. Denys, who had his head chopped off.

15. On June 21, Celtic priests gathered
16. to buy a left-handed screwdriver.

**ANSWERS:**

Line 1 and line 6 (see page 14), 3 and 12 (page 27), 5 and 16 (page 16), 7 and 2 (page 11), 9 and 4 (page 6), 11 and 14 (page 25), 13 and 10 (page 26), 15 and 8 (page 10).

# INDEX

First American Edition 1996 by
Franklin Watts
A Division of Grolier Publishing
Sherman Turnpike
Danbury, CT 06816

Franklin Watts Australia
14 Mars Road
Lane Cove
NSW 2060

Wilcox, Jane
   Why do we celebrate that? / Jane Wilcox
      p. cm. (Why do we?)
   Includes index
   ISBN 0-531-14393-7
   1. Holidays—Cross-cultural studies—Juvenile literature.
   2. Festivals—Cross-cultural studies—Juvenile literature.
   3. Fasts and feasts—Cross-cultural studies—Juvenile
      literature.     I. Title. II. Series.
   GT3933.W55 1996
   394.2'6—dc20                                      96—419
                                                     CIP AC

© 1996 Lazy Summer Books Ltd.  Illustrated by Lazy
   Summer Books Ltd.            Printed in Belgium

PRINTED IN BELGIUM BY
proost
INTERNATIONAL BOOK PRODUCTION

# EL GABILAN LIBRARY